CLUBMOOR REMEMBERS

. . . .
COMMEMORATING
100 YEARS
since the start of
WORLD WAR ONE
. . . .

BROAD SQUARE
PRIMARY
SCHOOL

FLORENCE MELLY
COMMUNITY
PRIMARY
SCHOOL

LEAMINGTON
COMMUNITY
PRIMARY
SCHOOL

ROSCOE
COMMUNITY
PRIMARY
SCHOOL

SPLICE
GROUP

ST. MATTHEW'S
CATHOLIC
PRIMARY
SCHOOL

CLUBMOOR
YOUTH
CENTRE

NORRIS GREEN
YOUTH
CENTRE

CLUBMOOR REMEMBERS
COMMEMORATING 100 YEARS SINCE
THE START OF WORLD WAR ONE

Contributors: the pupils of Broad Square, Florence Melly, Leamington, Roscoe and St Matthew's schools and members of Clubmoor Youth Club, Norris Green Youth Club and the Splice group.
Edited by Fiona Shaw
Design and production: Ken Ashcroft
Photography by Jack-All Productions
Additional photography by: Rhian Askins
Editorial assistant: Isabella Parry
Printed and bound in Italy by Graphicom.

ISBN: 978-0-9930221-1-1

First published in November 2014 by Wordscapes Ltd.
Second Floor, Elevator Studios
27 Parliament Street
Liverpool L8 5RN
www.wordscape.org.uk

CONTENTS

INTRODUCTION

WHEN Liverpool announced it was to host the Giants, and become one of the national centrepieces of World War One commemorations, people across the city were asked to do something. But in Clubmoor we have nothing to commemorate it with – there's no cenotaph here; no focal point.

So we thought about a focus for remembering the events of the Great War. Where would it go? Who would maintain it? How much impact would it have on the greatest amount of people?

We'd worked with the schools in the Ward before: they've always been enthusiastic and inclusive. And so the idea of a book came up, at a public meeting.

But World War One isn't really taught in junior schools. And we thought it was important that the children learn about the sacrifices that their great grandparents – and sometimes great great grandparents – made for us all. Fewer soldiers march every year at Remembrance Day. So who's going to tell them about it?

The four years of World War One had a dramatic, and often devastating, impact on people's lives. It affected every corner of their everyday existence – it separated families, changed the working day, affected food and education and toys. It changed the structure of life in this country forever.

Within that there was plenty to learn – and we were keen that the schools did different things, and each experienced it in their own way. They did so much – there were assault courses, wartime songs and drama lessons; arts and craft, baking bread, first aid and dressing up.

They were so open to it. They joined in everything with such enthusiasm. It is undoubtedly one of the nicest projects we've done in the area – seeing the children in the schools with some of our veterans, or listening to the Last Post, was incredibly moving.

And we wanted to keep that for them, which is why it's all in this book. It's a keepsake – a way of remembering forever the work they did, and what they got out of it. We all still have keepsakes from our childhoods – things we'll never throw away – and we hope this becomes one of theirs.

Clubmoor Remembers was funded by the Clubmoor Neighbourhood Fund, which is part of the Mayor's Fund in Liverpool. It's something we as Ward councillors use to try and give a bit back to the local community.

We're all so proud of every single one of them, and their teachers, who we couldn't have done it without. The enthusiasm of the schools and youth clubs, and their teachers and supporters, has made the project memorable for so many reasons.

This is about them.

IRENE RAINEY, ROZ GLADDEN AND JAMES NOAKES: CLUBMOOR WARD COUNCILLORS

LEST WE FORGET

ON 4 August 1914 Britain declared war on Germany, following its invasion of Belgium and Luxembourg.

Europe had been on the brink of war for many years: the continent was changing, with the unification of Germany and Italy in the 1870s, the declining influence of the Ottoman Empire (in what's now Turkey) and powerful, imperial Russia. Britain allied in the 'Triple Entente' with France and Russia; Germany, Austria-Hungary and Italy were bound by the 'Triple Alliance'. The shooting of the Austria-Hungarian Archduke Franz Ferdinand by a Serbian nationalist provided the spark that was to cause chaos across the continent for four long years; Austria-Hungary moved to invade Serbia, Germany supported them; war was declared.

Before war broke out, the King's Liverpool Regiment consisted of just two regular, two militia and six territorial battalions. One of the oldest infantry regiments in the country, it was formed in 1685 and – whilst most British army regiments were associated with a county – the King's Liverpool Regiment is one of only four that represents a city.

The huge recruitment campaign that started almost immediately after the declaration of war saw 49 battalions of the King's Liverpool Regiment involved over the next four years. Liverpool's battalions saw combat on the Western Front, Salonika and the North West frontier during World War One – some even sailed for Russia at the end of the war to fight against the Red Army in the Russian Civil War. But more than 15,000 of those Kingsmen were never to return home.

In August 1914, Lord Kitchener, Secretary of State for War, appealed for a 'New Army' of at least 100,000 volunteers. The idea of 'Pals' battalions was first proposed by General Henry Rawlinson

– he suggested that men would be more likely to join up if they were able to do so with friends, work colleagues and other local men. Lord Derby was the first to try it out, when he committed to raising a new battalion – of around 1,000 men – in Liverpool. In just days, enough men had signed up to form four battalions.

Those men became the 17th, 18th, 19th, and 20th battalions of the King's Liverpool – collectively they were known as the City of Liverpool battalions, or 'Liverpool Pals'. They were the country's first.

Other towns and cities joined in the great push for Pals, raising their own battalions. The competition between neighbouring towns and cities and the civic pride involved in the creating of Pals battalions led to a great wave of patriotism – by the end of August, around 30,000 men were enlisting every day, around the country. By mid-September 500,000 men had signed up; it was a million by the end of the year.

The Pals battalions spent 1914 and 1915 receiving training in the UK, before a planned offensive against the Germans in 1916 along the Somme river. The four Liverpool Pals battalions went to France in November 1915, before seeing their first battle during 'The Big Push' on 1 July 1916, the first day of the Somme Offensive. One of the longest and bloodiest battles of the First World War, more than one million men died at the Somme, including many members of the Pals battalions. Towns and cities across the country lost huge numbers of their men in a matter of days.

In total, 26 battalions of Liverpool's Kingsmen served overseas during World War One. Between them, they received 58 battle honours and six Victoria Crosses for their service on the Western Front, the Balkans, India and Russia.

We will remember them.

WORLD WAR ONE STATISTICS

World War One in numbers is based on research carried out in schools
as part of their commemoration project...

· · · · · · · · · ·

☞ **You had to be between 18
and 41** to fight in the war.
(AIDEN AND MORGAN, BROAD SQUARE)

· · · · · · · · · ·

☞ When war broke out in 1914
the British Army had
only **25,000 horses**.
(HOLLY AND SOLFELLA, BROAD SQUARE)

· · · · · · · · · ·

☞ **Horses were meant to carry
guns or ammunition.**
Britain used 467,973 horses.
(AIDEN AND MORGAN, BROAD SQUARE)

· · · · · · · · · ·

☞ In World War One they played
blow football. They were made out
of paper. They also played with toy
soldiers. They were were made out
of wood. The rag dolls were made
out of wood and fabric. They didn't
used to have battery toys then.
(JOEL, ST MATTHEW'S)

· · · · · · · · · ·

☞ **Veterinary officers** were
first appointed to the cavalry
regiments of the British Army in
1796 to reduce the huge loss of
horses experienced in earlier wars.
Without horses, the British Army
could not function. They were
vital for bringing in food and
ammunition, and for transporting
the wounded to hospital.
(HOLLY AND SOLFELLA, BROAD SQUARE)

· · · · · · · · · ·

☞ **Tanks were called landships**
but the British decided to call them
tanks. In World War One the first
tank was called Little Willie.
(ALEX, FLORENCE MELLY)

· · · · · · · · · ·

☞ **The most successful fighter** in
World War One was Rittmeister
von Richthofen. He shot down
80 planes – more than any other
World War One pilot.
(ALEX, FLORENCE MELLY)

· · · · · · · · · ·

☞ **65 million men** went to World War One and nearly ten million died. It is the sixth deadliest conflict in the world.

(ALEX, FLORENCE MELLY)

☞ By 1917, roughly 80% of the weaponry and ammunition used by the British army during WW1 was being **made by women** (munitionettes). Notably, women in the industry were paid on an average less than half of what men were paid. Munitionettes worked with hazardous chemicals on a daily basis without adequate protection. Many women worked with TNT, and prolonged exposure to the sulphuric acid turned the women's skin a yellow colour. They were popularly called 'canary girls'.

(CLUBMOOR YOUTH CLUB)

☞ By 1918 there were **20,000 Land Girls**. They milked cows, herded and ploughed, even thatched. In WW2 the Women's Land Army was re-established due to its success in WW1. And as its peak, there were 80,000 Land Girls.

(CLUBMOOR YOUTH CLUB)

☞ The Americans joined WW1 partly because the **Lusitania ship sank**. Over 100 Americans died. The Americans joined the war in 1917.

(FLORENCE MELLY)

BROAD SQUARE

PRIMARY SCHOOL

LEARNING
TOGETHER

DURING the World War One commemoration the children of Broad Square Primary, from nursery to year six, were involved in a number of events. We made and planted poppies, made bread and followed traditional World War One recipes. We contacted the Royal British Legion who imparted invaluable information about the role of the British Legion in remembrance. Children completed fabulous artwork, wrote their own poetry and letters and designed posters. The highlight was our attempt at making a human poppy which was aerially photographed. The children and staff were all thoroughly engaged in this three day event, learning invaluable lessons about the importance of remembrance and the ultimate sacrifice these brave soldiers made to secure our future.

ACTIVITIES:

- 1914 dining room
- created a giant poppy in the playground
- baked bread with poppy seeds
- had a talk from Liverpool veterans from the British Legion
- wrote diary entries
- listened to the Last Post
- learned wartime songs
- dressed in WW1 costume
- thought about soldiers before and after the war
- wrote acrostic poems
- made poppies

CLASS RS

CLASS RD

CLASS 2J

CLASS 2M

NURSERY CLASS (AM)

CLASS 1S

CLASS 1R

CLASS 4M

CLASS 5W

CLASS 5/6C

CLASS 6K

CLASS 4B

CLASS 3H

CLASS 3/4C

NURSERY CLASS (PM)

Broad square create a giant poppy out on the playground

Why aren't you fighting for your country?

why am you here

Niamh and Adam, year 1

Dear mum and dad,
I can see rats,
I can hear bombs.
It is cold.
I love you.
Love from Brooke.
xxx

*Brooke, year 1:
letter home*

Wilfred Owen

Che's portrait of Wilfred Owen

Holly and Solfella's 'war horse'

Dressing up fun!

Drama and dance

Year 1 WW1 classroom

Nursery in WW1 dress

WW1 writers

Letters home

Dance and drama

Lewis

Propaganda posters

Year 2 poppy display

Year 1

Nursery dress up as WW1 nurses

We will remember them
Our heroes are dying for us
Roads to glory risk lives
Lives were lost
Death is the only way out.

Winning takes time
Anything that can be risked must be
Risking your life, you will die in no man's land.

One life depends on another
Never let anyone shoot at you - shoot back
Ever after, it was all worth it.

Shoot back at the enemy
Our bullets are spraying to survive
Lots of blood pouring
Danger is fame
Incredible people are dead
Everyone is saved
Real people survived the war
Souls die for other souls.

Callum, year 5

☞ **A SOLDIER FIGHTS FOR OUR COUNTRY.** *There's lots of different kinds of armies.* **THEY WEAR CAMOUFLAGE ON THEIR COATS** *so they can blend in*

Eva, year 2

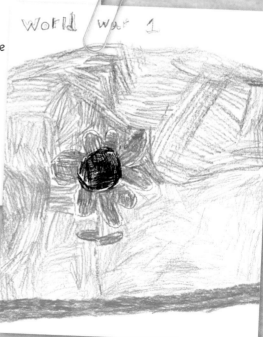

Emiliegh

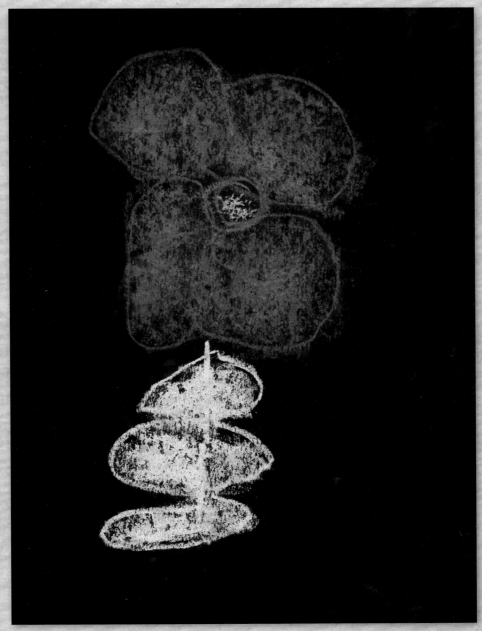

Poppies in chalk, by Daniel

Dear Mum
I do not like it out here it is horrible!!!
Loads of men have trench foot. I have to
poke the ugly lice! It is disgusting! There
are dead bodies everywhere I do not like it. Please
help me please!! The army men are sleepy. They are
sick of wwl. Some poor men have fleas because
they are very dirty. Big black mean fleas are trying
to eat our lovely nice clean food so we cover it.
Some men have fun.
                    Love Abi xxx

Lee, year 1

Abi, year 1: letter home

War LiFe WAr   Family now Family then

1. The Father was head of the Family
2. Many men chose to go out and fight in the war
3. More men were needed to fight in the war
4. You had to be in-between 18 or 41 to fight in the war
5. Children had been described to be seen and not heard
6. Teachers had rules they had to follow. For example
   they could not smoke, they could not go to an
   ice-cream parlour, they could not dye their hair, also
   they could not have any contact with men apart from
   their father or brother.
7. If one person in the class got a
   question wrong they had to stand in
   the corner with a pointy hat on.
   It had a D which means dunce.

WAr Family

Aiden and Morgan: fact-finding research

WORLD WAR LIFE

1. War changed children's lives – and their toys too. A toy cupboard in 1910 might have held a wooden hoop, a spinning top with a whip to make it whirl round, a skipping rope, a bag of glass marbles, a leather football, a rag doll or some painted toy soldiers and board games such as Snakes and Ladders or a new game of blow football. By 1914, people could buy Christmas crackers decorated with dreadnoughts (British battle ships). Shops offered toy machine guns and a board game about sinking German submarines, called Kill Kiel.

Men and boys often kept their coats, jackets and ties on, even in hot weather. People from every social class usually wore hats when they were outside. Children's clothes were usually miniature versions of grown up's clothes.

The seat was a hard narrow plank, often with no back. Benches were usually made for two people but sometimes up to 5 children sat at one. Children of different ages sat together in lessons. Often there were as many as 60 children in one class. If the school was large, boys and girls would be taught separately.

At the front would be a big wooden blackboard on a stand, on which the teacher wrote using a stick of chalk. The teacher's desk was often raised on a platform and teachers sat on tall chairs so they could watch the children at their desk. Near the teacher's desk was an iron stove with a coal fire during winter. The fires were often very small, even though the rooms were very big. In winter, children at the back shivered their way through class.

You had to be over 18 to be in the war and younger than 41. Also, as well as children having rules so did teachers and they were very strict ones, I promise.

With a fire lit every day in winter, the back room or living room was the only room that was really warm. Here the family sat in the evening and ate their meals. Only big houses had separate dining rooms. In a typical kitchen there was a gas cooker, sink and cupboards. Many kitchens had electric light, but there were no electric kettles, coffee makers, electric toasters, food mixers or microwaves.

Holly and Solfella: fact-finding mission

why aren't you fighting for your country?

Aisya and Ellie: propaganda poster

☞ *We wear poppies* **TO REMEMBER PEOPLE** *who have died*

Emiliegh, year 1

WILFRED OWEN!

Peter's Wilfred Owen

Nursery children dressing up

Sadie

Nursery children dress up in WWi costume

Louise and Rocco

More dressing up fun!

Peeping soldiers!

Megan and Aleesha

Callum

FLORENCE MELLY

COMMUNITY PRIMARY SCHOOL

WE were thrilled to be involved in such a fitting tribute to the heroes and heroines of World War One. It is especially important that the young people of today appreciate the sacrifices they made.

Our theme was family life. World War One was brought to life throughout the week. Children wrote letters, diary entries and newspaper reports. They learnt about the soldier's uniform and what life was like when your Father was at War.

The school as a whole made poppy bunting which was displayed on the yard, and in the dinner hall. On Monday lunchtime the children were served scouse and scones in line with the World War 1 Theme.

The week concluded with a War Time Picnic where classes commemorated the war with a minute silence. Songs, dance and dramas were also performed.

ACTIVITIES:

- drew poppies and made them from felt
- wore WW1 uniforms
- put on a play about the Christmas truce
- wartime picnic
- dancing collages
- built trenches
- first aid and bandages
- made Union Jacks
- joined in 'Dig for Victory' on their allotment, planting beetroot, cauliflower and turnip
- each class made a poppy wreath
- made poppy bunting

NURSERY CLASS 1

NURSERY CLASS 2

CLASS 1L

CLASS 1R

CLASS 2B

CLASS 2T

CLASS 3B

CLASS 3H

CLASS 4M

CLASS 4S

CLASS 5B

CLASS 5L

CLASS RH

CLASS RK

YEAR 6

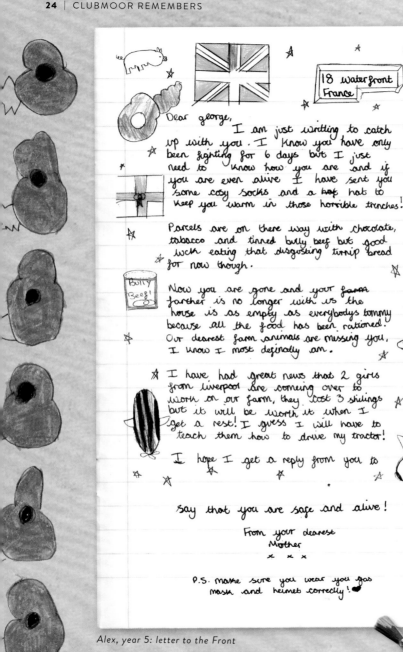

18 waterfront France

Dear George,
I am just writing to catch up with you. I know you have only been fighting for 6 days but I just need to know how you are and if you are even alive I have sent you some cosy socks and a hat to keep you warm in those horrible trenches!

Parcels are on there way with chocolate, tobacco and tinned bully beef but good luck eating that disgusting turnip bread for now though.

Now you are gone and your farther is no longer with us the house is as empty as everybodys tommy because all the food has been rationed. Our dearest farm animals are missing you, I know I most definatly am.

I have had great news that 2 girls from Liverpool are coming over to work on our farm, they cost 3 shilings but it will be worth it when I get a rest! I guess I will have to teach them how to drive my tractor!

I hope I get a reply from you to

say that you are safe and alive!
From your dearest
Mother
x x x

P.S. make sure you wear you gas mask and helmet correctly!

Alex, year 5: letter to the Front

poppies
by Mia

NEWS PAPER!
July 29th
1914!

**** WW1!

EMERGAINCEY

* * * WORLD WAR 1! * * *

The Wored War is out of our hands in the condition
it is in it might go on for longer than
this (Christmas) this war is going to be long
because of the way they are all getting more
soldures to fight and risk their lines.
This war is bringing more countries indanger
and inicent people are dying but with confedence
of fighting, being brave and a hero. While other
countries are getting more people we are fighting
farousiously because we don't need more people
we are the ones that are making them need more
killing them andwinning this war.
There are around 105 million soldures in this
war and half are on our side and there
are 10 million – 20 million that have died. R.I.P!

Amy, year 5

Nursery's giant wreath and
Reception's Union Jack

Aidan, year 2

Year 2 wartime performance

Stephen, year 1

Wartime picnic watching the WWI commemorations

Nathan, reception

Summer, reception

Children mesmerised with Miss Penny's war artefacts

Ethan (reception) with his poppy
for the class wreath

Nurse Olivia helping injured soldiers
Polly and Ewan

The trenches

It was horrible they had rats and nasty things in them. The food got eaten and pooed on by the nasty things. It made army men sick. I would be scared and miss you my family.

Kai, reception

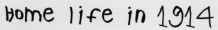

☞ *More than* **65 MILLION PEOPLE** *fought in World War One* **SO IT WAS A HARD BATTLE TO WIN**

Lucas, year 5

Tuesday 8th July 2014

Home life in 1914

Life was so different in 1914. We are comparing two different kitchens. In the 1914 kitchen it is old and dusty. There is a carpet in the kitchen. In the modern kitchen it is a lot different than the world war one kitchen. The sinks are very different because the sink in the world war one kitchen was like a tap. The sink in the modern kitchen is just like a normal sink.

Lilly, year 2

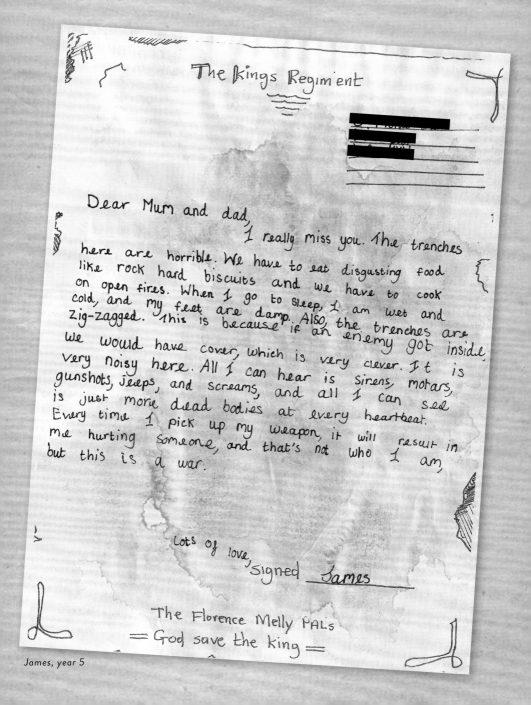

The Kings Regiment

Dear Mum and dad,

I really miss you. The trenches here are horrible. We have to eat disgusting food like rock hard biscuits and we have to cook on open fires. When I go to sleep, I am wet and cold, and my feet are damp. Also, the trenches are zig-zagged. This is because if an enemy got inside we would have cover, which is very clever. It is very noisy here. All I can hear is sirens, mortars, gunshots, jeeps, and screams, and all I can see is just more dead bodies at every heartbeat. Every time I pick up my weapon, it will result in me hurting someone, and that's not who I am, but this is a war.

Lots of love,
Signed *James*

The Florence Melly PALs
= God save the king =

James, year 5

8th July 1915

Liverpool Times

From this day on you may not see dairy products until the end of the war.

So now instead of flour, butter etc. we will be using vegetables such as turnips.

WE NEED YOU! To join the British army!

We've killed 13 million Germans and we wish to kill the rest.

Zeppelin shot down by the British army! They sought the opportunity as 14 men ganged up and repeatedly shot the zeppelin until it travelled to the ground like an autumn leaf just fallen from a tree!

The Germans struggle to get to France because of the distance the zeppelins can travel and the signs have been changed!

You Need To SMOKE!

Don't worry army men - rely on the women to get your clothes and weapons to France!

Smoking will calm you down during tough situations for instance the loud bombs and terrifying shrieks and all the rest. P.S. is it not bad for your health.

Amy, year 5

To my family.

I am terrified here.
I miss you so much.
It is raining so much.
People are dying every
day. It is horrible
here. I feel lonely
and upset. I feel
cross. I have bugs all
over me. It is scary.
        From Macy

Florence Melly

Bushey Road

Liverpool

L4 9VA

CLUBMOOR REMEMBERS

Macy, year 1

Tuesday 8th July

Home Life in 1914

Life was very different in
1914. In 1914 the people were
so poor. They did not have any
fridges or fruit or a washing
machine. Their house was very
dark because they did not have
any electricity. In 1914 they
didn't have any kettles because
in 1914 no one had any kettles.
The didn't have any new things
because there were no shops in
1914 and they were wearing old
dresses.

Somaia, year 2

The Great War was
1914-1918
First men put their
names into fight for
the families. They went
fighting and lots died.
They lived in trenches.
Trenches were wet and
dirty and muddy and smelly
and cold.

Shreya, reception

● ● ● ● ● ● ● ● ● ● ● ● ● ● ●
☛ **I DON'T THINK
WAR SHOULD
HAPPEN** *because
more people*
LOSE THEIR LIVES
every day
● ● ● ● ● ● ● ● ● ● ● ● ● ●

Max, year 5

Daniel, year 5

Dear my caring mum and Dad,

How is working in the Factory? you don't know how much I miss you! I wish I could see you all. I feel worried that I am going to die, you don't know how many guns are around me. When I go to sleep I can hear guns in my ears, but don't worry I will be fine.

Have you met any new Friends yet? if you have what are their names? I feel so sinister, I have shot 200 people already! I have nearly been shot but luckily I never! I have made a lot of new friends their names are Nathan, kevin, callum and michael they are all good friends, I only have four.

It is my birthday soon and I hope I am back home for it to celebrate it with all of my family and friends I am so excited for my birthday.

I am missing you!

lots of love from
Luke
ℓℓℓℓℓℓℓ

Tia, year 3: letter from the Front

Y4 World War One Acrostic Poem

Will we survive?
Our country needs us to fight.
Restless nights...
Leaving our families, hoping to return
Dreading the worst...

We will stick together – Proud to be British
Afraid but prepared to die for our country
Ready to make the sacrifice

Only one chance to make a difference
Never giving up, we soldier on
Everyone united, fighting for victory...

Class 4S, acrostic poem

. . . .
☛ **A POPPY**
is a symbol of
remembrance.
IT'S ALL
THAT WAS
LEFT ON THE
BATTLEFIELDS
. . . .

Josh, year 5

To my dearest mother,

All I can hear is bangs and screeching zeppelins crashing. As I rush outside to the Air Raid Shelter I grab my weapon the Flammenwerger M16. I go out to battle. I constantly have shivers up my arms and down my back. It's so scary I wish to be home eating your roast dinners instead of bully beef and turnip bread. I'm needed on the battlefield.

See you soon (hopefully)

Ben xxxx

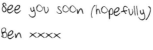

Keira's letter

LEAMINGTON

COMMUNITY PRIMARY SCHOOL

THE children of Leamington Community Primary participated in a week long 'Clubmoor Remembers...' project to commemorate World War One through a variety of tasks such as, writing letters, diary entries, creating poppy artwork, making bi-planes and lots more! Our children found this to be very informative and an enlightening experience. One that they will never forget!

ACTIVITIES:

- drama workshops
- WWI games – hopscotch, marbles, dominoes and snakes and ladders
- listened to radio shows about WW1
- built trenches in the classroom
- made bi-planes
- wrote letters to family at home
- WW1 assembly
- diary entries
- poppy artwork
- WW1 toys

MISS HIGGINS' CLASS

CLASS 1C

CLASS 1F

CLASS 2H

CLASS 2L

CLASS 3DC

CLASS 3JC

CLASS 4A

CLASS 4B

CLASS 5C

CLASS 5F

CLASS 6E

CLASS 6L

☞ **REMEMBRANCE DAY IS THE DAY** *when we put our hands together and* **REMEMBER THE PEOPLE** *that have died in the* **FIRST WORLD WAR.**

Aaliyah, year 6

War was a time of horror.
Over filled toilets flooded the trench
Rats were all over the place.
Lonely soldiers died of broken hearts
Death terrified the troops

Wives and children were worried
Armies had a truce at Christmas
Running soldiers were scared

On No Man's Land soldiers were pals
Never forget those brave men.
Everyone returned to their loved ones.

WILL YOU BE AMONGST THEM

BRITON NEEDS YOU!

Cameron, year 3

World War One
older people died in the war
red poppies represent the war
lots of people died in the war
dogs got sent to take messages

World War One had guns in it
austria was one of the countries that
russia fought in the war.

Old people starved in the war
nobody fought on Christmas
enemies played football

Class poem, year 3

Kevin's WW1 toys, year 1

WW1 workshops

Making our bi-planes

Creating poems!

Writing letters home

Molly's ID permit

Wayne and Chelsea

Having fun in the trenches

Lots of research was completed...

Caitlyn

We went to war!

Friday 4th July 2014   4.7.14
LoI can I write a World war one diary entry?

Dear diary,

Today dad sent us a letter he told us
that he was fine but some people had died
in the trenches! He also told us war was awful! He
asked us to knit him some socks because his
feet were sore. So mum went to work to earn
money for wool!

I have had to look after my little sister
because mum works for ages so I help her
cook and clean. To be honest sometimes I get
fed up of cleaning but I dont tell mum.
Today I made us all cabbage soup, I didn't
like it but I ate it anyway! My little sister
loved it She ate it all!

A few hours ago mum went to work so I
put my little sister to bed and now I'm getting
tired but nevermind. Mum works in a factory making
shells and a few bombs. Unusually her skin is
going yellow but she said it was alright! I have
a job of my own making posters about eating
less bread and growing your own vegtables!
I get paid half a crown which really helps mum!

Tomorrow school is open but mum says
I would have to stay off I needed to cook,
clean and care for my sister I am
sad but I have to help.

Anyway must get to bed its 8:30 mum
will be home soon, goodnight!

          Rio!
              xxxx

Rio, year 4

☞ *We buy poppies because* **THEY'RE THE ONLY FLOWERS THAT GREW** *after the First World War*

Luke, year 5

Aksen, Miss Higgins' class

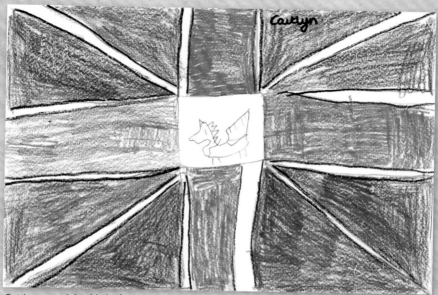

Caitlyn, year 6 (and below)

Dear family
I feel really broken without
you all. For months now I
have been in a state not
being able to wash or shave.
It's been really hard. I
mean, by the time I send
this letter and you receive
it I could be dead. These
trenches are really damp
and cold and we don't get
given much food. So we only
get one biscuit and chicken
stew. It will never beat yours
though.

From Henry

114 Southampton Road

Liverpool

England

L11

☞ *It would be* SCARY TO BE A CHILD *in the* FIRST WORLD WAR

Aaliyah, year 6

War is a horrible thing to fight for.

On Christmas both of the countries played football

red poppies in the field grow.

light is not out at night.

dark places are trenches and caves.

When football ended they started to fight.

a trench is what you hide in.

real danger is in a war.

On Christmas after football it ended. They fought.

no body cared

every body must remember

Alisha, year 3

Dear Archie,

I hate it here, it's appalling. It is not what the paper man makes it seem. It's terrible here. I want to come home and even worse, my best friend has died. Some people are lucky and they don't feel a thing because they die so quick but he was unlucky and died a slow painful death.

It was weird on Christmas Day. We all saw a German soldier on No Man's Land so we picked up our guns, we were ready to fire but he said "I come unarmed". We all put our guns down then more started, to have a kick about. On Boxing Day the fun stopped. We were fighting again so we all got kitted up and got into our trenches.

We are getting gassed by these new bullets recently. The German soldiers are firing them at us. We were terrified at first, the gas can make you go blind and your chest will sting like you would want to die.

I will tell you about trenches. They will make your feet go numb and rot because it's called trench foot. When you are sleeping rats nibble on your toes. I may not see you again I am injured. I miss you and love you. If I survive, I will be home soon.

Love from Walter

Paris, year 5

☞ **THE KIDS THOUGHT** *that World War One was really exciting,* **BUT THEY DIDN'T REALLY UNDERSTAND** *that it could end up* **IN A REALLY BAD TIME** *for other families.*

Rebecca, year 5

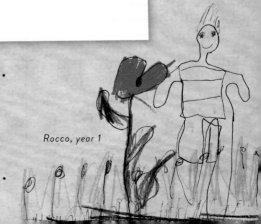

Rocco, year 1

World War One.

on Christmas Day

rats scurried through the trenches

late at night the rain poured down.

drafty sand bags broke inside the trenches.

When the soldiers pulled their triggers the sound went BOOM BOOM

all of the soldiers had to eat bully beef

rifles shot the people's heads

On the day after Christmas they started the war again

no one owns No Man's Land

everything stopped in 1918.

Callum, year 5

Cameron's poppies, year 3

Dear Mum and Dad,

I'm in the trench, it smells and it's dirty, but I can cope. I miss all of you, I can't wait to get home. I haven't caught any of the diseases yet but all my mates living with me have. I hope to see you soon lots and lots of love,
Charley
xxxx

CLUBMOOR REMEMBERS

23 Flint Road

England

Liverpool

L4

Postcards from the Front - Chloe, year 6

Dear Ashline,
Sorry I haven't written for a while due to the army. Anyway, how is my dear daughter Marylin? We have been sleeping in dugouts and you can fit 30 of us in it. It's a little cramped out at least it's warm! Rumour has it war is almost over. I doubt that could ever happen. We have been sitting in the trenches awaiting death for 2 years now, although being in the army isn't that bad. I even got to go in a tank today. It was amazing. I would also just like to say thanks for the packages. Tell Marylin I love and miss her and that goes for you too.
Lots of love from Edward

CLUBMOOR REMEMBERS

71 Flint Road

Norris Green

Liverpool

L4

Mollie, year 6

ROSCOE

COMMUNITY PRIMARY SCHOOL

SHARING
LEARNING
TOGETHER

IN July 2014, Roscoe Primary School went back in time 100 years to mark the outbreak of the First World War. The children learned about life both at home and on the battlefield. They studied books and saw photographs of soldiers and life at home during that time, and learned the importance of remembrance and the significance of the poppy.

It was important to us that the children should look beyond the activities and reflect on what life was really like for those involved. Year Four and Five pupils said: "World War 1 day was amazing. Our favourite part was going into the trenches and learning about what life would have been like in there."

ACTIVITIES:

- drama workshops
- writing on slates
- staff and pupils dressed up in Edwardian clothing
- creating 1914 classrooms
- playing games that children played 100 years ago
- finding out what it was like to be a soldier living in the trenches
- doing 'drill' with a soldier
- learning about life on the home front
- listening to music from 1914
- growing poppies

NURSERY CLASS (AM)

NURSERY CLASS (PM)

CLASS R1

CLASS R2

CLASS 1T

CLASS 12A

CLASS 2H

CLASS 3K

CLASS 4S

CLASS 5H

CLASS 6H

CLASS 6D

Tomas, 5H

Lois, 3K

Year 6
propaganda
poster

Antwone's propaganda poster, 4S

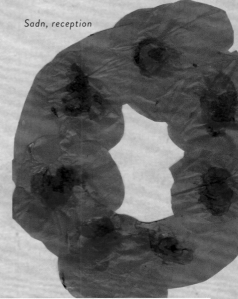

Sadn, reception

☛ I WOULDN'T LIKE
TO BE *a child in World
War One* BECAUSE I'D GET
FRIGHTENED *of all of the*
BOMBS CRASHING.'

Abigail, year 3

Amy, 5H

Ella, nursery

Lee, 4S

Biscuit making

Aimee, 3K

1914 classroom

Esther, 4S

Poppy wreaths

In the trenches...

Reception dressing up...

1914 classroom

Adam, 5H

Maths on slates

5H in the classroom...

Nursery make biscuits

Jake's wreath (reception) with Emilija's propaganda picture inside (5H)

Esther, 4S

Ellis, 5H

☞ *They would have been* **SQUASHED** *and it would have been* **NOISY** *with the* **BOMBS CRASHING**

Abigail, year 3

Francheska, 5H

BE in the Army

Remember the army

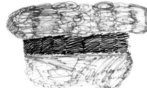

IF THE CAP FITS YOU JOIN THE ARMY

Year 6 work on their propaganda posters...

Britons

Wants you

Eva, 5H

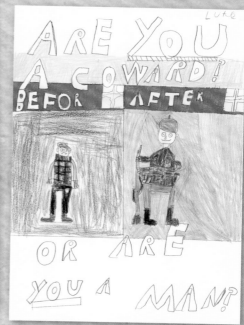

Luke, 5H

Jamie Leigh, 6D

☛ **WE WERE OUTSIDE** *on the playground building trenches and throwing bombs* **AND WHEN OUR TRENCH GOT KNOCKED DOWN I FELT A BIT SAD** *because the soldiers whose trench got buried or the bombs went in* – **THEY WOULD HAVE DIED STRAIGHT AWAY.** *When we did the same thing to the other team* **I FELT SORRY** *because if they had children back at home* **THEY WOULD HAVE LOST LIVES** *and* **THEY WOULD HAVE LOST THEIR FAMILY.**

Esther, year 4

Anthony (reception)

Ryan (5H) grows poppies

Lee on drill

Ellis, 5H

Roscoe Community Primary

Rolling out biscuits...

WW1 commemoration party

Morgan, 5H

Year 6 propaganda posters

SPLICE GROUP

CLUBMOOR Splice researched a number of different topics relating to WW1. This included uniforms, songs, games and food. We held a number of different evenings focusing on these topics. The group created a menu and prepared food which was served to all the group, making breads and stews which would have been the daily menu for our troops. The group wrote poems and drew pictures which were put on display within the centre.

Splice is a youth group for young people with disabilities aged between 13 and 19. It's designed to meet the needs of young people, promoting inclusion and raising awareness of issues around disability, while enabling young people to join in and participate in a range of activities including sports, art, music, drama and trips out. Splice gives them the opportunity to join projects and get involved alongside other young people, whilst making sure they're well supported and safe. Splice uses those activities to help build confidence, signpost new services and facilities and work towards training, employment and volunteering opportunities.

ACTIVITIES:

☞ dressed up in WW1 costume ☞ learned wartime songs ☞ practised marching ☞ made bread ☞ WW1 poems

Thanks to all of the members of Splice who were involved in the WW1 commemoration project:

Abbie, Adam, Alex, Ali, Ashley, Ben, Ben, Chloe, Claire, Edward, Eirin, Hannah, Hayley, James, Joe, John, Kaitlin, Kieran, Liam, Lisa, Mia, Rebecca, Richard, Shauna, Stephen, Susan, Teresa, Thomas and Tom.

Two of our young people hard at work in the kitchen

splice singing their hearts out

Propaganda poster based on research the young people did, by Joe and Claire

My Dad

My First Breath into
into the World Dad.
you wasn't there.
But my Mum promised.
Everynight that you would
always care.

Each day im growing
I'm starting to look like
you dad.
Mum always said you
loved me.
And dad I love you too.

When this war is
over dad.
you'll see the change
in me.
I can't wait for use to
come home.
to be with you Dad

A poem by two of Splice's young people, Hayley and Hannah

Edward leading the splice group in a medley of WW1 songs

Thomas joining in and dancing to WW1 music

Abigail and Suzanne making bread as part of their 'eating on rations' activity

The bread made by Splice's young people starts to take shape...

Shauna giving her army salute

Splice's giant group remembrance poppy

Cameras, lights, action!

Keeping focused in the kitchen...

Joe enjoying the blind scouse he helped to prepare...

Eddy does his solo

Playing the air raid siren game

ST. MATTHEW'S

CATHOLIC PRIMARY SCHOOL

TO commemorate the 100 year anniversary of World War 1, St. Matthew's R.C. primary school held a World War 1 history week. The week was based on two themes with Key Stage 1 finding out all about what school was like 100 years ago around the time the First World War started. The children really enjoyed getting a sense of what it would have been like in the classrooms through the use of role play, drama, creative writing, singing, dancing and art work. In Key Stage 2 the children looked at life in the trenches and wrote some heart-felt poems and letters capturing feelings and emotions at the time. The children developed a greater understanding of how this significant historical event had an impact on our country and lives.

ACTIVITIES:

- internet research
- made Union Jack flags
- assault course in the playground
- learned war-time songs
- made gas masks
- collages of war images
- themed WW1 lunch
- WW1 dressing up
- WW1 newspaper reports
- drama workshops
- WW1 poetry
- letters to the Front
- WW1 toys for children
- made a WW1 patchwork quilt and marching dance

YEAR 1

YEAR 2

YEAR 3

YEAR 4

YEAR 5

YEAR 6

June 1915

Dear Father
I really miss you I hope you are alright. Please don't worry because me and mother can look after each other. It has been horrid in school and the old selfish teacher hit me on the knuckles because she asked me to do my times tables and I didn't know them. The food in school is horrible and disgusting. Also I hate Pea Soup!!!! you only get four spoonfuls But I must not complain because I know that you only get tinned meat. Love from your daughter Sophie. xxx ♥

Sophie, class 2

Dear Diary,

The feeling what I have inside of me is horrible and sickening. Why did I apply for this? I am in a disgusting rat infested place where there is no place to hide! Not any more. I am desperate for some decent food and warmth! The sounds of the bombs exploding to the ground make me want to run, but I can't. I go solid stiff.

I cry myself to sleep at night drifting off thinking of my family who I might never see again! The saddest thing about this heartaching war is that I only got married to the love of my life a day before the war, and to think that I could die any minute without saying goodbye. Well it kills me. It really does.

Sophie, class 5

The one wish I would ask for is to be safe and for all this to go away. But it never does. I pray every night for myself to the Lord and for it to stop! Why can't it?

Just right now, this hour, one of my closet friends could be shot or even bombed. But just to think every second a man is being shot. I am one of the lucky ones. I will pray that all men stay safe. What would you do to stay alive? I am terrified!

The only person I can really talk to is you! I can't talk to anyone else because all of the men are manly and tougher, so I am alone in this hell like place...

☞ **REMEMBRANCE DAY** *is a day that we remember* **ALL THE SOLDIERS THAT DIED FOR US**

Elizabeth, year 6

Aidan (class 3A) tried out the assault course

Reception dress up...

Jack (reception) makes Union Jack flags

Harry, reception

Reception creates poppy wreaths

Faith (class 3) with our soldier's patchwork quilt

Olivia and Grace (class 1) making their gas masks

Class 1 trying out their gas masks

St Matthew's pupils enjoying their WW1-themed lunch

Faith, class 3

The Christmas Truce

List of characters:
John - British Soldier, blonde hair, Married, Kids.
Robert - German Soldier, brown eyes, Girlfriend, Kids.
David - British Soldier, young, Single.
Maliki - German Soldier, black hair, Married.
Dylan - British Sargent, Green eyes, black hair, single.
Tyrone - German Sargent, Green eyes, Married, Kids.

Scene 1

(Sitting in trench playing card games)(British trench)
Dylan: Right boys, I hope you're still up for battle?
David, John: Yes, Sir, yes!
Dylan: Well done boys, carry on.
David: SNAP! yes I won
John: Well done David, fair game.
David: I'm getting hungry. Are you?
John: Mmmm a bit.
Dylan: Dinner time. MMM today is ... SARDINE!
John, David: Ooooh yes!
Dylan: My gosh boys look!
John, David: What the?....

Scene 2

(German Soldier walks over)(then more)
Robert: Hello Tommy
(Everyone gets out of trench)
David: Would you like some chocolate?
Robert: Yes please
John: Hello Fritz
Tyrone: Hello Tommy
John: Could I interest into some brandy?
Tyrone: Oooh yes   I am thirsty
Maliki: Anyone up for a game of football?
Everyone: yes!

Scene 3

(A bomb is sent down)
John: Take this its my wife, Bonnie
Maliki: Thanks, heres my wife Hermione
Dylan: Bye!
(everyone runs back to trench)
Dylan: Have some rest busy day tomorrow!
The End   by Beth

Beth, class 5A

Christmas Truce 1914

Dear,
Mum, Dad and my little sister Lily,

I miss you. It's scary at war; However, I'm doing this to protect everyone from Germany. The mines are so dirty and dark. I feel like a pig covered in dirt. I nearly lost my leg from a bomb.

I have a great friend who I met called Bobby. He's so kind to me and we work together. We all wait in mines and then run as bombs drop like raindrops.

Moreover, I miss mums laugh and Lily giving me a hug every night. When will war end? I want to see you all again. Wish me luck!

Tell my friends that I miss them and I'll see them soon. I can't believe that I have been here for only two weeks! It seems like forever. God bless you all and I'll see you soon. I miss you all. All my love.
Ciara

Ciara, class 6

Toys during World War One
In World War One there was toy soldiers they were made out of wood. They also had rag dolls made out of cloth, they also had guns that were made out of plastic.

Callum, year 1

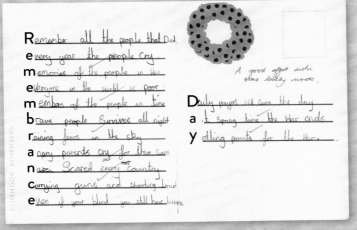

Remember all the people that Died
every year the people cry
memories of the people in war
everyone in the world is poor
members of the people in time
brave people Survives all night
raining fears in the sky
angry parents cry for their sons
nazi Scared every country
carrying guns and shooting loud
even if your blind you still have to work

A good effort with
some lovely words.

Daily prayers will save the day
at Spring time the War ends
yelling parents for the war.

Jessica, class 4

Dear Diary WW1

Dear Diary,

Today in school I learnt arithmetic, literacy and geography. When my friend was naughty miss gave him the dunce hat and the cane at the same time. Also because he was naughty he had to write " I will be good ". My Teacher is very mean and very strict because when she uses the cane she takes it very seriously. Our classroom is very cold and bare because we are very poor also we don't get enough good. There are very big holes in the walls and in winter we are very cold.

Thomas, class 2A

Sonny (reception) makes Union Jack flags

Harry (reception) making poppies

Heidi (class 4A) making silhouette artwork

Hannah and Jak (year 1) with the World War One class book

Faith and Sophie (year 3) with the soldier's patchwork quilt

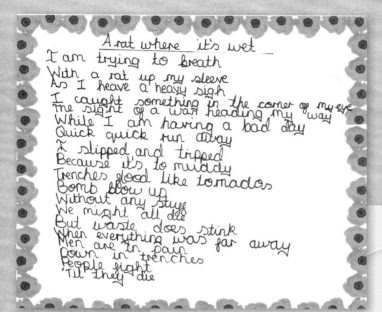

A rat where it's wet

I am trying to breath
With a rat up my sleeve
As I heave a heavy sigh
I caught something in the corner of my eye
The sight of a war heading my way
While I am having a bad day
Quick quick run away
I slipped and tripped
Because it's to muddy
Trenches flood like tornados
Bomb blow up
Without any stuff
We might all die
But waste does stink
When everything was far away
Men are in pain
Down in trenches
People fight
'Til they die

Faye Louise, year 4A

War war war,
what is it for.
killing everywhere,
no one will care.
Oh my god its war,
I cant believe what I have just saw
The war started 1914
England were very keen.
We faught and faught,
until the war ended,
England and their people defended.
England had a knife,
in one second they took a life.
War has begun,
it is the end of fun.
half of the people died,
all of the children cried.

Josh

Josh, year 6

CLUBMOOR YOUTH CENTRE

Liverpool Integrated
YOUTH AND PLAY
service

THE young people at Clubmoor Youth Centre thought about what aspects of WW1 that they would like to focus on, and participated in themes including the impact of war on women, how war influenced fashion, animals on the Front Line and poetry. As a result of their involvement they gained a sense of achievement and enjoyment, gained new skills and interests, and an awareness of the impact war has had on us today. They researched and communicated their ideas, and applied what they've learnt to these projects.

ACTIVITIES:

- ☞ researching and dressing WW1 wounds
- ☞ research into the impact of war on women's jobs
- ☞ how war influenced fashion
- ☞ research into animals used on the front line
- ☞ wrote war poetry
- ☞ wrote letters to and from the Front Line
- ☞ created their vision of the Giants coming to Liverpool
- ☞ created displayed based on our research

NORRIS GREEN YOUTH CENTRE

AS a group this was a really interesting project. We learnt some facts about what happened during WW1 and enjoyed searching for images that portrayed the Great War. We then drew and painted them onto our banner. We liked discussing and planning out the banner and working together as a team, and would like to do more projects like this in the future.

All work was done by David, Elisha, Lauren, Megan and Tim.

The young people researched the role of animals in the war

Wear a poppy

Wear a poppy on this day,
On the eleventh stand to pray.
And think about those who died,
and all the people who mourned and cried.

Wear a poppy on this day,
have two minutes silence, and then say;
Well Done! To those who held a gun,
until the deadly war was won

Wear a poppy on this day,
for several minutes stop your play.
Our soldiers didn't cower,
and they fought till their last hour.

So, wear a poppy on this day,
on the eleventh stand to pray.
And think about those who died,
and all the people who mourned and cried.

Hannah's 'Wear a poppy' poem

My darling Rose,

Hope all of you are well, our baby must be due to be born soon or it may have been. How is Jack and Emily? They must have you rushed off your feet. My darling I can't wait to be home in your arms once again.

Were all getting along here despite the crowded conditions. The rats are the worse, I can't get used to them like most of the boys. Thanks for the new socks you knitted for me, loads of socks are being given to the boys! I heard they have set up knitting clubs so that our feet can be dry most of the time.

I think of you everyday. I didn't think this dammed war would last this long. Think of me darling. I will write soon.

your loving husband. William
xxxx.

Letters from the Front

World War 1

The war the war what was it for?
Some of them were rich, some of them were poor.
Bombs, bullets, mud and and rats.
Poor dogs, poor horses and poor cats.

Dogs died and horses too,
There were diseases that made them go "achoo!"
The war was dangerous and sad,
It was sad, scary and very bad!

People didn't have a choice to go,
They had to say yes, not mayby or no.

By Emma

Boom! Bang!
Boo!   War!

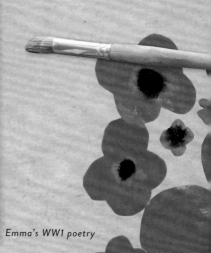

Emma's WW1 poetry

KEEP THE HOME
FIRES BURNING

Clubmoor Youth Centre members
research and plan their
commemorative artwork...

Penning WW1 poetry

keeping the home fires burning

World War One Cooking Workshop

. . . .

DIG FOR VICTORY was a response to a wartime problem of food shortages, but many of its outcomes reflect things we are concerned about today – having access to fresh healthy food, being active and living sustainably. The people of Britain were encouraged to grow as many fruit and vegetables on patches of land that were available including school grounds, parks and gardens. Communities were allocated allotments to encourage families to 'grow your own'. Root vegetables were easy to grow in the British climate, therefore were often used to produce stews, soups and broths. The young people attending Youth Group took part in a workshop and worked extremely hard, creating a Vegetable Root Soup using an authentic war time recipe and made some homemade bread loaves from scratch, feeding everybody who attended the celebration. Diners commented how delicious and wholesome the soup and bread tasted.

Keep the home fires burning

Clubmoor Youth Centre worked with local artist Michael Stainbury to create a series of WW1 displays. Their 'Keep the home fires burning' artwork commemorates the impact of war not only on the men who fought, but their family and friends at home, and wider society.

Dear Brother,

Please excuse my writing I can't stop my hand from shaking because I am so cold and terrified. I miss you and can't wait to hopefully make it home and see you. Hope you and the family is okay.

Lots of Love

Love

Letters to and from the Front

Dear uncle Joe,

I have been missing you loads, I haven't seen you for 3 years now. I hope you have been doing well and I wish to see you soon

My little brother has got his first 2 front teeth now!

We are all missing you

Love from

Amy-leigh

X X X X X X X X X

Curtis Watt from the Windows Project worked with CYC members on their poetry from the Front Line.

Dear Jack,

I hope you arer OK i miss you dearly and love you the world. mother has fallen gravely ill. and may not live to see the daylight tomorrow. all of the family wish you the best is has been 3 years now and we all know you'll be able to survive a few more.

Lots of Love
your baby
sister
Mia
xxx

Mia's letter to the Front

Sergeant Stubby

Stubby Stubby always grubby
Stubby Stubby standing proud
Stubby Stubby guns are so loud
Stubby Stubby, little legs to get under things
Stubby Stubby this is what war brings
Stubby Stubby never thought I'd be
Stubby Stubby in trench mud up to my knee
Stubby Stubby I'd luv to be
Stubby Stubby chasing cats up and down
    the alley
Stubby Stubby lying by a nice warm fire
Stubby Stubby your mum is so proud
Stubby Stubby good things in small packages
Stubby Stubby a whistle blowing that's
    my cue
Stubby Stubby of they only knew

Poet Curtis Watt worked
with Clubmoor Youth Centre
members on their WW1 poetry

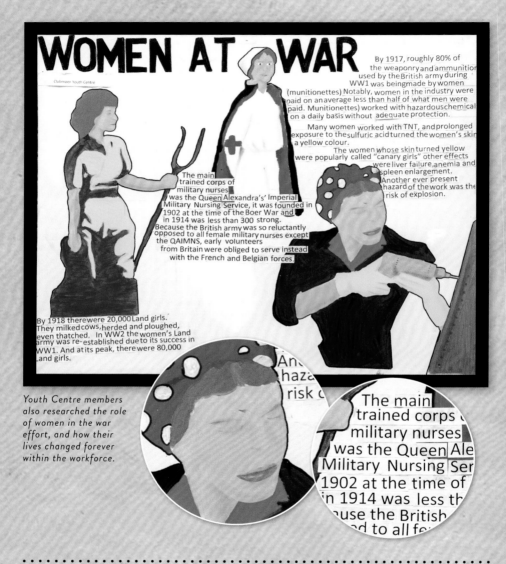

WOMEN AT WAR

Clubmoor Youth Centre

By 1917, roughly 80% of the weaponry and ammunition used by the British army during WW1 was being made by women (munitionettes) Notably, women in the industry were paid on an average less than half of what men were paid. Munitionettes) worked with hazardous chemical on a daily basis without adequate protection.

Many women worked with TNT, and prolonged exposure to the sulfuric acid turned the women's skin a yellow colour.

The women whose skin turned yellow were popularly called "canary girls" other effects were liver failure, anemia and spleen enlargement. Another ever present hazard of the work was the risk of explosion.

The main trained corps of military nurses was the Queen Alexandra's' Imperial Military Nursing Service, it was founded in 1902 at the time of the Boer War and in 1914 was less than 300 strong. Because the British army was so reluctantly opposed to all female military nurses except the QAIMNS, early volunteers from Britain were obliged to serve instead with the French and Belgian forces.

By 1918 there were 20,000 Land girls. They milked cows, herded and ploughed, even thatched. In WW2 the women's Land army was re-established due to its success in WW1. And at its peak, there were 80,000 Land girls.

Youth Centre members also researched the role of women in the war effort, and how their lives changed forever within the workforce.

The main trained corps of military nurses was the Queen Ale Military Nursing Ser 1902 at the time of in 1914 was less th use the British d to all fe

The main trained corps of military nurses was the **QUEEN ALEXANDRA'S IMPERIAL MILITARY NURSING SERVICE,** *it was founded in 1902 at the time of the Boer War and in 1914 was less than 300 strong. Because* **THE BRITISH ARMY WAS SO RELUCTANTLY OPPOSED** *to all female nurses except the QUAIMNS, early volunteers from Britain were* **OBLIGED TO SERVE INSTEAD WITH THE FRENCH AND BELGIAN FORCES.**

I Lied

I lied, I lied - I lied about my age
I'm trapped, I'm trapped - I'm trapped
without a cage
There's bombs, there's bombs -
Bombs, blood and fire

Oh. how I wish I would not have
been a liar!

BOM, BOMB,

By
Katie

Katie's WW1 poem 'I lied'

Little war horse

Little war horse galloping through
    no man's land
Little war horse missing bombs
    and bullets.
Little war horse carrying men
    and guns,
Horses struggling, horses lying.

Little war horse saving lives.
Little war horse ready to die.
Little war horse unstable to ride,
Trembling through the mud and flies.

Little war horse why oh why?
Little war horse you chose
    this life.
Little war horse are you ready
    to die?
Here comes the bullet.
    Say goodbye.

Megan's 'Little war horse'

Norris Green's members hand-painted a giant Clubmoor Remembers banner

Norris Green youth centre members concentrate on the details on their banner

Norris Green Youth Centre members did a variety of research before starting work on their banner, including reading original WW1 newspapers

The commemorative banner starts to take shape

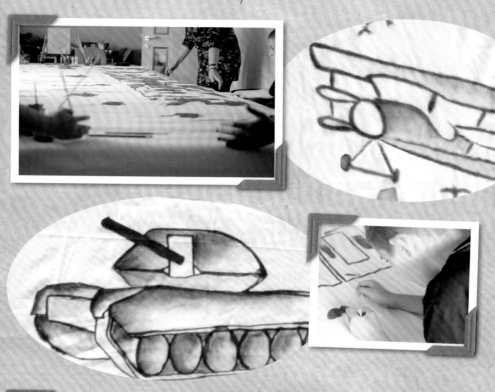

THANKS

WE would like to express our gratitude to the many people who have helped with our World War One Commemoration Project.

A special thank you to Pauline Bibby from Liverpool City Council, who led the project from start to finish and spent many hours coordinating the group behind the scenes, keeping the project together and on track.

A big thank you to all those who provided support, talked things over, read, wrote, offered comments, and participated in the drama workshops which the children truly enjoyed. Zain Salim, you captivated the children in your sessions with your passion for drama; Michalle Wright, your cookery lessons were a revelation. Thanks to Curtis Watt at the Windows Project for his poetry workshops, and to Michael Stainbury for the art sessions that took place at Clubmoor Youth Centre, both of which were supported by LMH.

The enthusiasm of the schools and youth clubs, their teachers and supporters, has made the project memorable for so many reasons. A special big thank you to the following teachers and youth leaders, who agreed to lead for their individual schools and groups. Without your hard work and commitment our project would not have been possible.

- Carolyn Whitehead, Broad Square Primary School
- Anna Reeves, Florence Melly Community Primary School
- Ashley Fergusson, Leamington Community Primary School
- Stephen Harper, Leamington Community Primary School
- Rachel Davidson, Roscoe Community Primary School
- Carmel Rush, St Matthew's Catholic Primary School
- Pauline Daly, SPLICE Disability Group
- Anita Farmer, Clubmoor Youth Centre
- Glenn Campbell, Norris Green Youth Centre

Many thanks also to Kelly Forshaw and her team at Jack-All Productions, who filmed the project with our schools and groups. Your professionalism and the keenness you all brought to the project is evident within the DVD, together with the comments made by the children.

A big thank you to Fiona Shaw and her team at Wordscapes, who have guided us in the process of design, material selection and publishing our book. Your patience and guidance has been instrumental to get our book to print.

Last and not least, to all of the pupils within our five schools and members of our youth centres whose names are too many to mention. We couldn't have done it without your enthusiasm – we hope you enjoyed taking part in the project, and learnt the importance of the remembrance of the Great War.

PRIMARY SCHOOL SPLICE GROUP ST. MATTHEW'S CATHOLIC PRIMARY SCHOOL CLUBM
Y PRIMARY SCHOOL LEAMINGTON COMMUNITY PRIMARY SCHOOL ROSCOE COMMUNIT
EN YOUTH CENTRE BROAD SQUARE PRIMARY SCHOOL FLORENCE MELLY COMMUNITY
UP ST. MATTHEW'S CATHOLIC PRIMARY SCHOOL CLUBMOOR YOUTH CENTRE NORRIS G
N COMMUNITY PRIMARY SCHOOL ROSCOE COMMUNITY PRIMARY SCHOOL SPLICE GRO
ARE PRIMARY SCHOOL FLORENCE MELLY COMMUNITY PRIMARY SCHOOL LEAMINGTON
RIMARY SCHOOL CLUBMOOR YOUTH CENTRE NORRIS GREEN YOUTH CENTRE BROAD S
HOOL ROSCOE COMMUNITY PRIMARY SCHOOL SPLICE GROUP ST. MATTHEW'S CATHOL
RENCE MELLY COMMUNITY PRIMARY SCHOOL LEAMINGTON COMMUNITY PRIMARY SC
YOUTH CENTRE NORRIS GREEN YOUTH CENTRE BROAD SQUARE PRIMARY SCHOOL FLO
Y PRIMARY SCHOOL SPLICE GROUP ST. MATTHEW'S CATHOLIC PRIMARY SCHOOL CLUBM
Y PRIMARY SCHOOL LEAMINGTON COMMUNITY PRIMARY SCHOOL ROSCOE COMMUNIT
EN YOUTH CENTRE BROAD SQUARE PRIMARY SCHOOL FLORENCE MELLY COMMUNITY
UP ST. MATTHEW'S CATHOLIC PRIMARY SCHOOL CLUBMOOR YOUTH CENTRE NORRIS G
N COMMUNITY PRIMARY SCHOOL ROSCOE COMMUNITY PRIMARY SCHOOL SPLICE GRO
ARE PRIMARY SCHOOL FLORENCE MELLY COMMUNITY PRIMARY SCHOOL LEAMINGTON
RIMARY SCHOOL CLUBMOOR YOUTH CENTRE NORRIS GREEN YOUTH CENTRE BROAD S
HOOL ROSCOE COMMUNITY PRIMARY SCHOOL SPLICE GROUP ST. MATTHEW'S CATHOL
RENCE MELLY COMMUNITY PRIMARY SCHOOL LEAMINGTON COMMUNITY PRIMARY SC
YOUTH CENTRE NORRIS GREEN YOUTH CENTRE BROAD SQUARE PRIMARY SCHOOL FLO
Y PRIMARY SCHOOL SPLICE GROUP ST. MATTHEW'S CATHOLIC PRIMARY SCHOOL CLUBM
Y PRIMARY SCHOOL LEAMINGTON COMMUNITY PRIMARY SCHOOL ROSCOE COMMUNIT
EN YOUTH CENTRE BROAD SQUARE PRIMARY SCHOOL FLORENCE MELLY COMMUNITY
UP ST. MATTHEW'S CATHOLIC PRIMARY SCHOOL CLUBMOOR YOUTH CENTRE NORRIS G
N COMMUNITY PRIMARY SCHOOL ROSCOE COMMUNITY PRIMARY SCHOOL SPLICE GRO
ARE PRIMARY SCHOOL FLORENCE MELLY COMMUNITY PRIMARY SCHOOL LEAMINGTON
RIMARY SCHOOL CLUBMOOR YOUTH CENTRE NORRIS GREEN YOUTH CENTRE BROAD S
HOOL ROSCOE COMMUNITY PRIMARY SCHOOL SPLICE GROUP ST. MATTHEW'S CATHOLI
RENCE MELLY COMMUNITY PRIMARY SCHOOL LEAMINGTON COMMUNITY PRIMARY SC
YOUTH CENTRE NORRIS GREEN YOUTH CENTRE BROAD SQUARE PRIMARY SCHOOL FLC
Y PRIMARY SCHOOL SPLICE GROUP ST. MATTHEW'S CATHOLIC PRIMARY SCHOOL CLUBM
Y PRIMARY SCHOOL LEAMINGTON COMMUNITY PRIMARY SCHOOL ROSCOE COMMUNIT
EN YOUTH CENTRE BROAD SQUARE PRIMARY SCHOOL FLORENCE MELLY COMMUNITY
UP ST. MATTHEW'S CATHOLIC PRIMARY SCHOOL CLUBMOOR YOUTH CENTRE NORRIS GF
N COMMUNITY PRIMARY SCHOOL ROSCOE COMMUNITY PRIMARY SCHOOL SPLICE GRO
ARE PRIMARY SCHOOL FLORENCE MELLY COMMUNITY PRIMARY SCHOOL LEAMINGTON
RIMARY SCHOOL CLUBMOOR YOUTH CENTRE NORRIS GREEN YOUTH CENTRE BROAD S
HOOL ROSCOE COMMUNITY PRIMARY SCHOOL SPLICE GROUP ST. MATTHEW'S CATHOLI
RENCE MELLY COMMUNITY PRIMARY SCHOOL LEAMINGTON COMMUNITY PRIMARY SC
YOUTH CENTRE NORRIS GREEN YOUTH CENTRE BROAD SQUARE PRIMARY SCHOOL FLC
Y PRIMARY SCHOOL SPLICE GROUP ST. MATTHEW'S CATHOLIC PRIMARY SCHOOL CLUBM
Y PRIMARY SCHOOL LEAMINGTON COMMUNITY PRIMARY SCHOOL ROSCOE COMMUNIT
EN YOUTH CENTRE BROAD SQUARE PRIMARY SCHOOL FLORENCE MELLY COMMUNITY
UP ST. MATTHEW'S CATHOLIC PRIMARY SCHOOL CLUBMOOR YOUTH CENTRE NORRIS GR
N COMMUNITY PRIMARY SCHOOL ROSCOE COMMUNITY PRIMARY SCHOOL SPLICE GRO
ARE PRIMARY SCHOOL FLORENCE MELLY COMMUNITY PRIMARY SCHOOL LEAMINGTON
RIMARY SCHOOL CLUBMOOR YOUTH CENTRE NORRIS GREEN YOUTH CENTRE BROAD S
HOOL ROSCOE COMMUNITY PRIMARY SCHOOL SPLICE GROUP ST. MATTHEW'S CATHOLI
RENCE MELLY COMMUNITY PRIMARY SCHOOL LEAMINGTON COMMUNITY PRIMARY SC
YOUTH CENTRE NORRIS GREEN YOUTH CENTRE BROAD SQUARE PRIMARY SCHOOL FLC
Y PRIMARY SCHOOL SPLICE GROUP ST. MATTHEW'S CATHOLIC PRIMARY SCHOOL CLUBM
Y PRIMARY SCHOOL LEAMINGTON COMMUNITY PRIMARY SCHOOL ROSCOE COMMUNITY
EN YOUTH CENTRE BROAD SQUARE PRIMARY SCHOOL FLORENCE MELLY COMMUNITY
UP ST. MATTHEW'S CATHOLIC PRIMARY SCHOOL CLUBMOOR YOUTH CENTRE NORRIS GR